CONTENTS

INTRODUCTION

Arthur Kelly, age 68, worked for 10 years for the Grand Valley Tool & Die Corporation in Millville, Ohio, in the 1970s. He remembers that he was part of a pension plan that, as a young worker, he had paid little attention to. Now, he has just retired from his most recent job. He has a small pension from that employer, along with Social Security benefits, but he could use additional income. He wants to track down his old employer and start collecting whatever pension money he is owed. But when he calls the company's old number, he finds it is "not in service." A call to the phone company's directory assistance for Millville draws a blank—Grand Valley Tool & Die is not listed. He is at a loss. How can he find out if he still has a pension?

Arthur Kelly is a fictitious person, but his problem is all too real. Thousands of retired workers in the United States are entitled to pension payments that they have not claimed because they do not know where to look. After all, a private company may:

- move from one city or town to another;
- close down a particular plant or office to consolidate its operations elsewhere;
- be bought by another company and given a new name;
- merge with another company;

1

- divide into separate parts, none of which retains the old company name;
- go bankrupt;
- any combination of the above; or
- simply close its doors and disappear.

Workers may be tempted to shrug their shoulders and write off the pensions as "lost." Indeed, some pensions may in fact be gone forever. In many cases, though, the pension money is sitting safely in a fund, waiting only for the worker (or a surviving spouse or beneficiary) to come forward to collect it. If you think you may be entitled to money in a pension fund, either as a participant or as a spouse or beneficiary of a participant, it makes sense to try to track it down. This booklet, which is based on the experience of pension counselors, gives advice on how to plan and conduct your search. A glossary (Appendix A) explains some terms that may be unfamiliar.

DEFINING YOUR SEARCH

First, Is It Worth Looking?

Vesting. The most important question to ask yourself at the outset is whether your work for this past employer entitled you to a pension. Another way to put this question is this: Were you vested in the pension plan at the time that you left the job? Being vested means that, no matter when you leave the job, you are eligible for a pension at retirement age. You may have left the job 20 years ago, but if you were vested, you are entitled to pension benefits. Even if the pension fund no longer exists, you may still be able to get your pension benefits. (See the box on page 8 about "Legal Protections.")

 Today, most pension plans require five years of service, or employment, before vesting. But before the mid-1980s, plans typically required 10 years and, before the mid-1970s, 20 years or more. Before 1976 plans could even require that you keep working for the same employer until you actually retired to get a benefit. If you don't know for a fact that you were vested in the pension plan, and you only spent a few years on the job before the mid-1980s, the chances are slim that you are entitled to a benefit.

Rules of Eligibility. Every private pension plan's rules of eligibility are contained in a document called a summary plan description (SPD) that is supposed to be given to every worker at the time he or she joins the plan. As the rules change, the worker should periodically receive an updated document. The rules in effect at the time you leave the company are the rules that determine whether you have a pension or not. Changes in the rules after you leave the company usually do not apply to you.

 Summary plan descriptions were required only after Congress passed the Employee Retirement Income Security Act (ERISA) in 1974. In some cases, however, comparable company documents are available for earlier years, especially in the case of pension plans that were developed in negotiations between management and a union.

When You Left Matters. If you left a job (which provided a pension) after 1975, you have more rights under federal law than if you left earlier (see the box on page 8 on "Legal Protections"). However, even if you left a job before ERISA became effective for your pension plan, you may still be able to collect your pension if you can locate the pension fund and you met the requirements for a benefit before you stopped working for the company.

Spouses' Rights. Defined benefit ("traditional") pension plans must provide married workers with a qualified joint and survivor annuity (QJSA). A QJSA entitles the worker's spouse to a benefit if the worker dies after retiring. If the QJSA is not waived (see below), and the spouse survives the worker, pension payments will continue, usually at a reduced amount, for the rest of the spouse's life. In addition, since August 23, 1984, defined benefit plans have been required to provide preretirement survivor coverage that would provide a benefit to the spouse if the worker dies before retiring.

Before 1985, many pension plans offered joint and survivor options but often a worker could choose a different benefit form without his or her spouse's consent. Beginning in 1985, defined benefit plans were required to pay married workers a joint and survivor benefit unless the worker waived this form of payment and the spouse consented to this change in writing. If you are a surviving spouse, it may be worth looking for a pension your husband or wife may have earned regardless of when he or she left the job.

For a definition of "defined benefit plan" see Appendix A: Glossary.

What You Are Looking For

The object of your search is the pension plan—or its successor—that may owe you a benefit. Broadly speaking, here is what may have happened to your benefits:

- The plan may still be intact, in one form or another. That is, the original company may have reorganized, or been bought out, but the current owners have inherited the legal obligation to pay the benefits due under your old pension plan.

- The plan may have bought an annuity contract from an insurance company that took over the obligation to pay annuities to people entitled to benefits under the plan.

- The plan administrator may have arranged for a financial institution or other company to administer the plan, or transferred the money owed to workers who could not be found to a financial institution.

- The plan may have been taken over by the Pension Benefit Guaranty Corporation (PBGC), which will pay the benefits up to certain limits (see box on page 13).

- The plan may have been terminated by the employer, with benefits paid to plan participants who could be found. If the plan was a defined benefit plan, benefits for "missing" participants like you may have been turned over to PBGC for its Pension Search Program. (See box on page 13.)

- A final possibility is that the plan is simply gone, along with the money it owed. This possibility, although it is usually illegal, cannot be ruled out. But there is no reason to assume that it happened.

 Your job will be to trace the history of the pension plan from the time you left the job to the present. This may be as simple as finding

out where your old company has moved, or it may be as difficult as piecing together a complicated story of corporate mergers and bankruptcies. The sources of help described on pages 14-23 may well be necessary in your search.

Legal Protections

Once, private pensions were almost entirely unregulated. It was not at all uncommon for a worker to reach the end of a long working life and find that his or her nest egg, in the form of an ample pension, had completely disappeared. In 1974 Congress passed the Employee Retirement Income Security Act (ERISA). This law, and other reforms enacted since 1974, established broad protections for many workers. The Department of Labor monitors pension plans to make sure they are solvent and are being responsibly managed. The Internal Revenue Service (IRS) also regulates pension plans, primarily for tax purposes.

ERISA established PBGC, a federal agency that insures private defined benefit pension plans, to make sure that workers are not deprived of their accumulated benefits (see page 13 for more information on PBGC). However, not all pension plans are protected by this federal law. Here are the major exceptions to ERISA's safeguards:

- Only private-sector workers are protected, not employees of the federal government or state or local governments.

- The ERISA protections are not retroactive: that is, they do not apply to workers who left their companies prior to the effective date of ERISA. For most plans the effective date is 1976 but for some plans, especially those established after ERISA was passed, the effective date might be as early as 1974. For multiemployer plans, the effective date may be later. Nonetheless, in some cases, a person who left a job before that time might be due a benefit, if he or she satisfied the provisions of the plan for a benefit and was vested in the benefit when he or she left the job.

- PBGC only insures defined benefit pension plans (see Appendix A for definition and ERISA §4021(b) for a listing of the types of defined benefit plans not covered by PBGC.)

GETTING READY TO SEARCH:
LOOKING FOR
DOCUMENTS

You should gather any documents you can find that may have a bearing on your pension eligibility and keep them in one place. Any or all of the following types of documents can be valuable:

- a notification that you are vested in the plan;
- an individual benefit statement (which many larger plans provide automatically each year);
- an exit letter, received when you left, noting your participation in a pension plan;
- a summary plan description showing the plan's rules, including the rules for vesting.

Documents showing the full official name of the company and its Internal Revenue Service ID number can also be helpful, in case you need to trace what happened to the company. Any documents that show your period of employment and your earnings while working for the company will also be useful to prove your eligibility after you have located the plan. Such documents include pay slips and W-2 forms.

 If you contact the Social Security Administration, you can get a copy of your "earnings record," which will show how much you were paid each calendar year by each employer. From that record, you may get your employer's federal ID number, which may be helpful in tracking down the plan. Call

1-800-772-1213 and ask for Form SSA-7050, entitled "Request for Social Security Earnings Information." (You can also get a copy of the form and its instructions by going to the Social Security Administration's Web site at **www. socialsecurity.gov/online/forms.html**.) This form will show whatever fees you may need to pay for the information. You should expect that the response from Social Security may take six weeks or more.

YOUR POTENTIAL ALLIES
IN THE SEARCH

Looking for a pension fund can be confusing. For that reason, once you have gathered as much of the information mentioned above as possible, it is important to look for guidance where you can find it. Here are some potentially helpful allies.

The U.S. Department of Labor

ERISA gave the Department of Labor a major role in protecting the pension rights of workers in the private sector. Within the Department, the Employee Benefits Security Administration (EBSA) and EBSA's regional and district offices provide assistance to individuals who are having difficulty with their pensions. (Addresses and phone numbers for the EBSA offices are listed in Appendix B.)

The benefit advisors are experienced in all aspects of ERISA. They can provide you general information about your rights and will intervene with administrators of the fund on your behalf if necessary. They can also assist you in your search for a "missing plan."

The Pension Benefit Guaranty Corporation

PBGC maintains an online listing of people who are entitled to benefits from certain pension plans but who cannot be located. (See the box on page 13.) The PBGC list constitutes a potential shortcut for some workers or their beneficiaries looking for pensions that may still be owed them.

Pension Counseling Projects

Through grants from the U.S. Administration on Aging, a number of free pension counseling services were initiated in the 1990s.

They provide free pension counseling to individuals in their service areas. Many specialize in difficult situations, including those in which people are unable to locate their pension plans. A number of states, including some of the largest ones, have such counseling services. (Names, addresses and phone numbers of these projects are listed in Appendix C.)

Public Libraries

Most libraries will have resources—printed directories and online data bases—that can help in your search. The directories may be helpful in tracing a company: for example, the library may have directories listing acquisitions and mergers going back a number of years. Workers at the reference desk can help you use these sources, and they can help you find free or low-cost private clearinghouses for unclaimed retirement benefits. In most cases, they can also help you use one of the library's computers in your search.

The Pension Benefit Guaranty Corporation

PBGC provides a possible shortcut to finding your lost pension if:

- you had a defined benefit pension plan that terminated after July 1, 1974 (a defined benefit pension plan promises participants specified benefits at retirement, with the benefits generally based on such factors as salary, length of service, and age at retirement); **and**

- the sponsor of your plan was a private company that was not a religious organization, nor was it a professional service employer (such as lawyers, doctors, and architects) that employed 25 or fewer persons. The PBGC will not be able to help if your plan was paid for only by union dues or was administered by a government agency.

You can access (or have someone access for you) PBGC's online listing at **www.pbgc.gov/search/default.htm**. Or, you can find this listing by going to PBGC's Web site at **www.pbgc.gov**, clicking on the "Workers and Retirees" tab at the top of the page, and then clicking on the link under the heading "Pension Search: Help us find missing participants." As of 2009, PBGC's listing identified about 37,000 people who had pensions waiting for them. Even if your name does not appear in this listing, you may wish to check the list of plans taken over by PBGC to see if PBGC is now responsible for a plan you were once in. The list may be viewed at **www.pbgc.gov/trusteedplans/default.htm**.

The technology involved is simple. If need be, a librarian at your local public library should be able to find the site and look for the information within a matter of minutes. You (or someone else) can simply type in your last name to find out whether you are on the list of "lost" participants. You can also type in the company's name to see if its pension plan has been taken over by PBGC.

If you do not have computer access you may write to the PBGC Pension Search Program, P.O. Box 151750, Alexandria, VA 22315-1750.

PLACES TO LOOK

First and foremost, keep in mind the "Allies" discussed in the previous section. Start with a search of PBGC's database, which covers all participants in terminated defined benefit plans who could not be located by PBGC or by their former employer. If this fails, contact the federal Department of Labor and pension counseling projects for guidance in your search.

But these are not the only places to look. In this section, we discuss ten possible sources of information on the whereabouts of your pension. Some of them are easier to use than others.

 Even if the sources of information described in this section do not lead you directly to the pension fund, small steps can be enormously helpful. If you find out the name of a company that bought your old employer, for example, then you can use the other sources to look for that second company. (To find a pension plan, you will normally need to find the company that sponsored it, even though the plan and the company are not the same thing.)

1. If you can easily get in touch with any former co-workers who stayed at the company longer than you did, they may be able to tell you what happened to the company. If the former co-worker is getting pension checks, ask where the checks are coming from.

2. A union that represented workers at the company (even if you yourself were not part of the bargaining unit) may have information. Other workers may have asked the union the same question.

If you don't know which union it was, or how to locate it, the state's labor federation (the state AFL-CIO) may be able to help you identify and find it. The labor federation is likely to have its office in the state's largest city or its capital city.

3. The Chamber of Commerce of the city or town where the company was located may know where the company moved, or who bought it out. If the first person you talk to doesn't know, ask if they can refer you to someone who has been active in the Chamber over a long period of time.

4. In some cases, the name and address of the pension plan administrator, as listed in the most recent document you can find, may lead you directly to your answers. If the address is different from the company's old address, there is a chance that this person will still be reachable there and can either end your search or can help you with it.

Every pension plan has someone—or some department—officially designated as the plan administrator. In a very small company, it is likely to be the owner who functions as the plan administrator. In a bigger company, it is usually another executive or a pension benefits department. It could also be someone from an independent firm that specializes in handling pension plans. In any case, the plan administrator keeps the employment and pension records for each participant in the pension plan. If the pension plan is still intact, then the plan administrator is the object of your search.

5. The plan's annual financial reports may identify the plan's accountant, actuary, trustee or attorney. One of these parties should be able to tell you who can provide up-to-date information on the plan. These reports are contained in federal Form 5500; they are filed with the Employee Benefits Security Administration (EBSA) about two years after the year that they cover, and they are kept by the EBSA for six years. For information, call a benefits advisor on EBSA's toll-free hot line (1-866-444-3272) or e-mail EBSA through the Web address: **askebsa.dol.gov**.

6. A specialized business library may be able to provide information about a corporate merger or buyout that affected your company. One in particular, the Kirstein Library (a branch of the Boston Public Library), has been very helpful and is not limited to Massachusetts

companies or callers from Massachusetts. Its address is 20 City Hall Avenue, Boston, MA 02108 and its phone number (8 am – 5 pm, Monday-Thursday; 9 am – 5 pm Friday and Saturday) is 617-523-0860.

7. An Internet search for information may be helpful. There are several "search engines" that enable someone to type in the name of a company, perhaps with other key words, and gain almost instantaneous access to relevant information. A librarian at your public library is likely to know how to use one of these searching techniques.

 Keep in mind that the computerized searches suggested here are an easy matter for someone—a librarian, a relative, a friend—who is familiar with finding information on the Internet. In many cases, searching for documents that contain both the name of a company and the word "pension" will retrieve relevant information. In many other cases, of course, it will not yield anything helpful. But it is worth a try. It may be especially helpful if you have been able to trace your company's trail through one or more name changes or corporate mergers.

8. Your state government requires annual reports from corporations—reports that, among other items, list the names and addresses of the

corporate officers. The responsible state agency may be the Secretary of State's office or it may have another name. A call to the main switchboard of your state capitol building should give you the name and phone number of the agency that collects these reports. In some cases, contacting one of the corporate officers listed in the report may be important in finding out what happened to the company.

9. If the company was publicly traded, a stock broker may know what happened to it.

10. If you find out that the company went bankrupt, try to get the name and address of the trustee in bankruptcy.

In a great many cases, a lost pension plan can be located—and locating it can mean tangible benefits for the participant, spouse, or beneficiary who is owed money under the pension plan. However, it is hard to tell which of these sources will provide the necessary information, and sometimes none of them will work. Even experienced pension counselors will sometimes have to abandon hope of finding a lost pension.

WHAT TO DO IF
YOU FIND THE
PENSION FUND

If you find the company (or its successor), you will then have to find out what happened to the plan. You are likely to end up in contact with one of these potential holders of your pension money:

- The plan administrator of your pension plan (or of another plan with which yours has been combined).

- An insurance company to which the plan administrator transferred funds in the plan for the purpose of providing annuities to eligible participants.

- A financial institution in which accounts were established for participants who could not be paid because they could not be located.

- PBGC, if it took over your pension plan's obligations, or if your defined benefit plan was terminated and its plan administrator used PBGC's missing participants program when it couldn't find you.

Regardless of which of these has the pension money, your approach to them—your next step—should be similar.

Initial Contact

Contact the plan administrator, the insurance company, the financial institution, or PBGC, giving your dates of employment and offering to provide a copy of the most recent individual benefit statement that you have. Ask if you were covered and what benefits you are entitled to. Ask for a copy of the summary plan description. If the party you contact responds that you are not entitled to a pension, you can read the document to see whether you agree with that decision or not.

 Any correspondence should be sent by a delivery method that provides confirmation of delivery (e.g., a return receipt).

If You Are Not Satisfied

Insurance company. If it is an insurance company that controls the pension fund, then the initial response it provides is fairly certain to be its final response. An insurance company, at the point when it takes responsibility for a plan, accepts the employer's records regarding (a) who the participants in the plan are and (b) what benefits each participant is entitled to. The same is true for financial institutions in which accounts were established for participants who could not be located. If you have documents or other evidence that the information relied on by the insurance company or financial institution is incorrect, it's likely that you will have to go back to the employer to make your case that the information is incorrect.

PBGC. If PBGC has taken over the pension plan, it also accepts the employer's records but its initial determination regarding an individual's benefits is subject to an appeal process.

Ongoing plan. If the pension plan is still intact (or has been combined with another employer—sponsored pension plan) you also have the possibility of recourse. If the plan administrator says you are not eligible for a pension but you aren't convinced, or if the pension benefits do not seem to add up to what you are entitled to, then you should get advice. The best initial sources are:

- The Employee Benefits Security Administration (EBSA) of the U.S. Department of Labor (see Appendix B).

- A pension counseling project if there is one in your area (see Appendix C).

  An EBSA benefit advisor or a pension counselor can look over your records and advise you as to whether you have been given fair treatment. If you haven't, they can give you free assistance in getting the benefits to which you are entitled. They may intervene on your behalf with the plan administrator and will advise you about, or assist you in following, the plan's appeals procedure if necessary.

Other Sources of Help

If you should decide you need a lawyer to represent you, the National Pension Lawyers Network maintains a list of attorneys, in all 50 states, that handle pension claims. The Network can be reached at (617) 287-7324 or (617) 287-7332, by e-mail at **npln@ umb.edu**, or through its Web site at **www.pensionaction.org/npln.htm**. Before deciding to take on the expense of a lawyer, however, you should satisfy yourself that the amount of money that is potentially involved is worth the cost.

The American Academy of Actuaries maintains a pension help registry consisting of actuaries willing to volunteer to help people check the accuracy of pension calculations. This list may be accessed through their Web site at **www.actuary.org/palprogram.asp**. The Academy is at 1100 17th Street NW, 7th floor, Washington, DC 20036, and can be reached by phone at (202) 223-8196 or by e-mail to **actuary@actuary.org**.

The national Pension Rights Center (1350 Connecticut Avenue NW, Suite 206, Washington, DC 20036) can be reached by phone at (202) 296-3776. Or, you can e-mail them through their Web site at **www.pensionrights.org/contact**.

A FINAL WORD

This booklet provides help in defining, planning, and conducting a search for a "lost" pension. There are no guarantees of success. Perhaps the only certainty is that, if you make no effort to locate the pension fund, whatever money may be owed to you will never be yours.

APPENDIX A:
GLOSSARY

Defined benefit plan: A type of pension plan that promises participants specified benefits at retirement. The benefits usually are based on the number of years worked for a company or in an industry, and they may also be based on salary during that time. The employer is responsible for maintaining enough money in the pension fund to meet the plan's obligations, usually the payment of a monthly annuity to the plan participant and survivor benefits to that participant's spouse.

Defined contribution plan: A plan in which the employer and/or the employee put money into the individual account of the employee but no specified benefits are promised at retirement. The employee is entitled to the amount of money put into his or her account, adjusted for any income, expenses, gains or losses posted to the account. These plans have become increasingly common in recent years; examples include profit-sharing and 401(k) plans.

EBSA (Employee Benefits Security Administration): Agency within the U.S. Department of Labor whose responsibilities include the regulation of pension plans.

ERISA (Employee Retirement Income Security Act): Federal law passed in 1974 that tightened the standards for the administration and funding of pension plans and gave regulatory powers to three federal agencies: the Department of Labor, the Internal Revenue Service and the Pension Benefit Guaranty Corporation. A number of subsequent amendments and laws since 1974 have strengthened ERISA's protections.

Multiemployer plan: A collectively bargained plan maintained by more than one unrelated employer, usually within the same or related industries, and a labor union.

PBGC (Pension Benefit Guaranty Corporation): A federal corporation established under ERISA to insure private-sector defined benefit pension plans. PBGC takes over the payment of pension benefits in cases where corporate sponsors of defined benefit pension plans have gone bankrupt, ceased operations, or proved to a bankruptcy court or to the PBGC that the plan sponsor cannot remain in business unless the plan is terminated.

Plan administrator: The person or persons who administer the plan. If no one is designated as the administrator in the plan document, the employer is considered to be the plan administrator. The plan administrator is responsible for maintaining the pension plan, keeping records on individual participants, overseeing the payment of benefits under the plan, and managing the plan assets.

Vesting: The point at which a participant becomes permanently entitled to a benefit under the terms of the plan at retirement age, whether or not he or she continues to work for the employer. A pension plan will specify the length of service required for vesting. A participant who has satisfied vesting requirements is said to be "vested."

APPENDIX B: EMPLOYEE BENEFITS SECURITY ADMINISTRATION (EBSA)

U.S. Department of Labor
EBSA Office of Participant Assistance
200 Constitution Avenue NW, Room N5623
Washington, DC 20210
   Toll-free hot line: 1-866-444-EBSA (3272)
   Web site: **www.dol.gov/ebsa/**

District Offices

Detroit District Office
211 W. Fort Street, Suite 1310
Detroit, MI 48226-3211
   (313) 226-7450

Miami District Office
8040 Peters Road, Bldg. H, Suite 104
Plantation, FL 33324
   (954) 424-4022

St. Louis District Office
Robert A. Young Federal Bldg.
1222 Spruce Street, Room 6310
St. Louis, MO 63103
   (314) 539-2693

Seattle District Office
1111 Third Avenue, Room 860
Seattle, WA 98101-3212
   (206) 553-4244

Washington District Office
1335 East-West Highway, Suite 200
Silver Spring, MD 20910
    (202) 693-8700

Regional Offices

Atlanta Regional Office
61 Forsyth Street, Suite 7B54
Atlanta, GA 30303
    (404) 302-3900

Boston Regional Office
JFK Building, Room 575
Boston, MA 02203
    (617) 565-9600

Chicago Regional Office
200 W. Adams Street, Suite 1600
Chicago, IL 60606
    (312) 353-0900

Cincinnati Regional Office
1885 Dixie Highway, Suite 210
Ft. Wright, KY 41011-2664
    (859) 578-4680

Dallas Regional Office
525 South Griffin Street, Room 900
Dallas, TX 75202-5025
    (972) 850-4500

Kansas City Regional Office
2300 Main Street, Suite 1100
Kansas City, MO 64108
   (816) 285-1800

Los Angeles Regional Office
1055 East Colorado Boulevard, Suite 200
Pasadena, CA 91106-2341
   (626) 229-1000

New York Regional Office
33 Whitehall Street, Suite 1200
New York, NY 10004
   (212) 607-8600

Philadelphia Regional Office
Curtis Center, Suite 870 West
170 S. Independence Mall West
Philadelphia, PA 19106-3317
   (215) 861-5300

San Francisco Regional Office
90 7th Street, Suite 11-300
San Francisco, CA 94103
   (415) 625-2481

APPENDIX C:
PENSION COUNSELING PROJECTS

Mid-America Pension Rights Project
(866) 735-7737
(KY, MI, OH, PA, TN)
http://www.mid-americapensions.org/

Michigan Pension Rights Office
Legal Hotline for Michigan Seniors
3815 W. St. Joseph's Street, Suite C200
Lansing, MI 48915
   http://elderlawofmi.org/pension_rights_project/index.html
   Toll Free: (800) 347-5297
   Local: (517) 485-9164

Ohio Pension Rights Office
Pro Seniors, Inc.
7162 Reading Road, Suite 1150
Cincinnati, OH 45237
   www.proseniors.org/oh_pension.html
   Toll Free: (800) 488-6070
   Local: (513) 345-4160

Mid-Atlantic Pension Counseling Project
(NJ, NY)

New York Pension Rights Office
South Brooklyn Legal Services
105 Court Street
3rd Floor
Brooklyn, NY 11201
   http://www.sbls.org/index.php?id=253
   Toll Free: (800) 355-7714

New England Pension Assistance Project
(CT, MA, ME, NH, RI, VT)

New England Pension Assistance Project
Gerontology Institute
University of Massachusetts, Boston
100 Morrissey Boulevard
Boston, MA 02125-3393
   www.pensionaction.org
   Toll Free (New England): (888) 425-6067
   Local: (617) 287-7307

South Central Pension Rights Project
(AR, LA, MO, OK, TX)

Texas Pension Rights Office
Texas Legal Services Center
815 Brazos, Suite 1100
Austin, TX 78701
   www.southcentralpension.org
   Toll Free: (800) 443-2528

Upper Midwest Pension Rights Project
(IA, MN, ND, SD, WI)

Iowa Pension Rights Office
Iowa Legal Aid
1111 Ninth Street, Suite 230
Des Moines, IA 50314
   www.iowalegalaid.org
   Toll Free: (800) 992-8161
   Local: (515) 282-8161
   Fax: (515) 244-5525

Minnesota Pension Rights Office
Minnesota Senior Federation
1885 University Avenue West, Suite 190
St. Paul, MN 55104
    www.mnseniors.org/content/category/17/64
    Toll Free: (866) 783-5021
    Local: (651) 783-5021
    Fax: (651) 641-8969

Western States Pension Assistance Project
(AZ, CA, HI, NV)

California Pension Rights Project
California Senior Legal Hotline
444 North Third Street, Suite 312
Sacramento, CA 95811
    http://www.seniorlegalhotline.org/
    Toll Free: (866) 413-4911
    Local: (916) 930-4911

www.ingramcontent.com/pod-product-compliance
Lightning Source LLC
Chambersburg PA
CBHW070730180526
45167CB00004B/1695